A LETTER

TO

My Lord * * * * * * *

ON

The PRESENT DIVERSIONS
of the *TOWN*.

(Price Sixpence.)

A LETTER

TO

My Lord *******

ON

The *Present Diversions* of the TOWN.

WITH

The *True Reason* of the DECAY of our DRAMATIC ENTERTAINMENTS.

Thunder and Lightning now for Wit are play'd,
And shortly Scenes in Lapland will be laid:
Art Magic is for Poetry profess'd,
And Cats and Dogs, and each obscener Beast
To which Ægyptian Dotards once did bow,
Upon our English *Stage are worship'd now:*
FLETCHER's *despis'd,* JOHNSON *is out of fashion,*
And Wit the only Drug in all the Nation.

DRYDEN.

LONDON,

Printed for J. ROBERTS, near the *Oxford-Arms*
in *Warwick-Lane*. M.DCC.XXV.

MY LORD,

IT would be impoffible to refift your kind Invitations to the Country, if I was not fix'd here by a Neceffity, which I was never angry with before. Tho' the Pleafure of your Seat, and the more exquifite Delight of your Lordfhip's Company, would be a fufficient Excufe for leaving any Bufinefs: I am afraid now, your Lordfhip will be fo unkind to attribute it rather to the Gaiety of my Temper, (which You always faid I had enough of,) and my

B   Love

Love for our *Town-Amusements* : No, my Lord, believe me, they are not so dear to me at present, and except the *Opera*, there is scarce one, I can find any tolerable satisfaction in.

THE *Masquerades*, I own, would be agreeable to me, were they as they ought to be; but we never had the proper *Humour* for them, or if we had, it is entirely lost: A Man of *Wit*, and uncommon *Vivacity*, might make and find *Entertainment* there indeed; but we have so very few, who shine in that *Light*, that they are duller than the dullest of our other Diversions: That sullen Love for good Sense, (the Distinction of our Nation,) and the Fear, lest we should be betray'd to speak any thing else, makes us appear more absurd than we should be in acting any ridiculous *Character* to the Life; so that three parts of us you see gaping, like *Shirley* in the *Rehearsal*, and at a very great loss what to do or say.

say. The others find, as they say, their Pleasure in *Intrigues* : But the Expence might be sav'd, since they are as well carried on in the *Drawing-Room*, or even in *Places* sacred to *Devotion*. When that Devil the Spirit of Intriguing is once acquainted with a Woman, he can attend her any where; and *Hypocrisy* at *Church* is found to be as good a Disguise, as a Mask at the *Theatre* : If *your Lordship* remembers the pleasant Story you told me of Lady *F——*'s Amour at the *Chappel*, it will justify me in what I say.

OUR *Opera's* indeed are in perfection ; we have a Composer or two, and two Singers, that cannot be excell'd, if rival'd by any in the Universe. But yet I have a Complaint against them; them I cannot say, but against our immoderate Love for them. *Your Lordship* will be surpriz'd to hear me say so, as you have always con-

demn'd

demn'd my Fondness for them ; I own,
my Lord, the Charms of *Musick*, and
doat on them ; I can dwell on the de-
lightful Tone of SENESINO'S Voice, or
attend to the pleasing Extravagancies of
our little Warbler CUZZONI, with as
much Rapture as any one, and more,
I believe, than most People : But however it is with grief I see *Music* banish
every thing else from our Discourse, it
is with regret I see our *Fidlers* look'd
on as the first *Genius's* of our Nation,
and that a Man must make *Harmony*
his Study to be fashionable in Company. You know, I never went to
White's for Conversation, but it is the
same with our Men of Wit, and Letters : Those, who can judge of a VIR-
GIL, or point out the Beauties of a
SHAKESPEAR, sacrifice that Delight to
the more agreeable Talk of *Fuges*,
Counterfuges, *Divisions*, &c. Your
Lordship will laugh at this, I am sen-
sible, but it is true ; we are as great
Pedants in *Music*, as any the *Uni-
versity*

verfity can produce in the *Claffics*. Yet even this might be tolerable in thofe, who are Judges of it; in thofe, who have a delicate Ear, and Tafte: but the Infection reaches farther, even to them, who are entirely ignorant of the *Science*, who have no Relifh for it, no Satisfaction in it, who are weary of an *Opera*, before it is half finifh'd; and thefe generally, if not always, make a great part of the *Audience*.

But yet, this is not all; it has help'd to banifh the *Mufes*: the *Mufes*, who feem'd fond of being among us, and had taken up their Refidence at our other *Theatre*, are gone, or will foon be driven thence; tho' I know not why they fhould difagree, they are Sifter Arts, have both their Charms, and both tend to civilize and refine us; with this difference to the advantage of the latter, that, while it pleafes, it teaches us to regulate our Paffions for the future, but the other only calms them for the prefent.   But

BUT however, *my Lord,* I will not charge the Difcouragement that *Poetry* lies under, wholly here, nor will I (as it commonly is,) attribute it to the vitiated *Tafte* of our *Nobility* and *Gentry:* No, furely it is their Intereft to fupport it. Every one, who is ambitious of being a *Polite Man,* muft make it his Defire to encourage that, which will fooneft render him fo. *Poetry* has ever had this *Character:* 'Tis to that we owe, that AUGUSTUS, from a rough and cruel Tyrant, was chang'd into a humane, and generous *Prince.* 'Tis to that,————but it is needlefs to give more Inftances; its Charms were never difputed, there never was a perfect *fine Gentleman,* or *truly great Man,* but was a Lover of it.

A TASTE is as fure a Diftinction of a Gentleman, as his *Behaviour,* and a much happier one, than his *Quality:* This

This creates him Respect only among the lowest of Mankind, That commands it even from the highest. It is a proof of the Greatness of a Man's Wit, as well as his Soul, since it requires a Capacity to judge, and Generosity to judge with Candor : It scorns the low Entertainments of narrow Minds, who are delighted with any thing that glitters; it enquires into the real Merit of every thing, and values nothing without it : It is founded on good Sense, yet good Sense alone will not give it; it must be form'd by conversing familiarly with our best *Authors*, by frequently seeing and reading the best of their *Performances*, and closely attending to their various Beauties, so as to make them our own.

Now too, methinks, after the late handsome Example of our KING and *Ministry*, for the promoting and enlarging our *Learning*, it should be unfashionable

fashionable for any Man of Character to be negligent in it.

An Spes & Ratio Studiorum in Cæsare tantum?

No, we have, I am perfuaded, many Men of Figure like *your Lordfhip*, who have a juft Tafte, and high Value for every thing, that is elegant, and we have (I believe) or may have *Genius's*, that would be no Difgrace, nay perhaps might be an Honour to any Man, who would be at the trouble to look them out, and patronize them.

Your Lordfhip will wonder now, why *Poetry* fhould be in fuch contempt on the Stage : as I am no *Poet*, I may poffibly be miftaken ; but from my own Obfervation, and the Talk of my Acquaintance, I fancy I can give a plain Reafon for it.

It is not, my Lord, owing to any open Attacks without, but to the Treachery

chery of its pretended Friends within:
We have three Men, who call themselves the *Managers* of our *Stage*, who
have gone further towards its Ruin,
than the united Attempts of all its
Enemies could have done : Of these
we have one who is a perfect *Draw-
canfir* in his way, declares open War
against every thing, that has any Merit
in it, assaults both Friends and Foes,
(if he is capable of having either,) dif-
obliges all the World, and then defies
them for their Contempt of him : He
has always made a very good Fop, and
from thence pretends to judge of Nature it-self: He is a good *Buffoon*, and
acts a *Villain* very justly, therefore
assures himself, that he is qualify'd for
a *Critic*, or a *Tragic Writer*. How
he appears in the last View, you can
determine by his late *Performance*,
where by the way your Lordship thinks
very right, that by the help of COR-
NEILLE, LUCAN, and the *Opera Writer*, he has produc'd a Piece, that would

C   be

be a scandal to the worst of them. Yet this Man (the *World* says, I own I have no knowledge of him otherwise) sits as Judge on every Play, that is brought to them, expects they should be submitted to his Alteration; and to this Man it is owing, that we have had nothing new this Winter but his own, and that I cannot send your Lordship, (what I was put in expectation of, by four or five of the first Taste,) two or three Plays that would be pleasing to you.

To him and his Companions we are indebted for the loss of SHAKE-SPEAR, OTWAY, and CONGREVE: Loss I call it, since they drive from the House every Person of Figure and Capacity, by adding their *Absurdities* (which they call *Entertainments*,) too low for Men of Sense to see, and since the Crowd, which are diverted with them, cannot enter into the Beauties of our Authors: Their Excuse for

this,

this, is, their Bufinefs is to get Money; it may feem a prudential Reafon to them, but at the fame time it is a convincing one, why our Men of Power fhould take notice of them, and curb their Prefumption. That there is fuch a Power over them, is certain; for the Honour of being HIS MAJESTY's Servants, is the only thing, that exempts them from being accounted *Vagrants*; I do not therefore fee, why they look on themfelves as their own Mafters, and that they have a Power to impofe on the Town, as they think fit.

WIT has not been for fome time at a lower Ebb than at prefent; the *Theatre* is the Fountain-Head of it, and if a ftop is there, it muft run fhallow every where elfe, and will continue to do fo, while thefe People are fuffer'd to affume to themfelves the Power of cenfuring as they pleafe: for it cannot be thought, a Man of any *Genius*, who has been at the trouble

C 2

and

and care of forming a *Play*, will fub-
mit it to the *Infolence* of their refufal,
or the *greater Infolence* of their offer-
ing to correct it. And it is no new
Complaint againft them, that they have
refus'd *Pieces*, which have had the
Applaufe, and the Recommendation
of the beft *Judges*, (as particularly I
remember fome Years ago one of
Mr. YOUNG's,) without any tolerable
Reafon for it: Their Reafon could not
be, becaufe they were bad ; for that
would have influenc'd them againft a
great Number of *thofe*, which they
have acted fince, and efpecially the
laft.

YOU are furpriz'd, I know, at my
unufual Serioufnefs on this head: Believe me, *my Lord*, except the Love
of my deareft Charmer Mifs . . . .
and *your Lordfhip's* Company, (on my
word it is no Flattery, *my Lord*,) there
is nothing gives me fo exquifite a *Delight*, as a well-written and well-acted
Play,

Play. I think it so fine an *Entertainment*, that it is with the greatest sorrow I see the Decay of our *Stage*; and since one of the best Proofs a Man can give of his *Politeness*, is his Taste of these various Drawings of *Nature*. I am fearful lest we should, by our Neglect of them, degenerate into Ignorance, and *Stupidity:* Besides, I have been long of *your Lordship's* opinion, that an *Elegance* in Thinking is one of the best Preservatives against the Corruption of our *Morals*. I cannot therefore, I confess, with any patience see a *Harlequin*, or *Scaramouch* usurp that *Stage*, where I have been so often delighted with the Distresses of OTHELLO and JAFFIER: Where I have seen *Nature* in its greatest Beauties, I cannot without resentment see these *Fopperies* of a *Smithfield Booth*. Nor can we hope for better, while the Direction is in these *Creatures*; who, govern'd by their Ignorance and Interest, would rather fill their Houses with Fops, Prentices,

tices, and Children, than Men of the
firſt Diſtinction and Senſe, who (as I
told your Lordſhip,) have by their Ab-
ſence ſhewn their juſt Contempt for
theſe *Fooleries*, which yet have been
forc'd on the *Town* by the *Managers*,
who have had the Boldneſs beſides (as
you ſaw in the *Prologue* to Cæsar,)
to tell them, they were agreeable to
their *Taſte*.

Nay, among thoſe, who crowd to
the ſight of them, there are Numbers
that hiſs them every time they are pre-
ſented; which is an undeniable proof,
that there are few, who ſee them a ſe-
cond time, and that there is a juſt Taſte
ſtill remaining: yet the *People* of *Fa-
ſhion* are reproach'd for what they de-
ſpiſe.

I Would not by any thing here in-
ſinuate ought againſt their worthy In-
ſpector Sir Richard St——le, who
has deſerv'd more of the World than
moſt

most Men, by his Endeavours to refine
our Thinking, and give us a true No-
tion of *Merit* : Besides, he has always
been an Enemy to these. *Trifles*, and
has shewn by his own *Comedies*, that
we may be entertain'd with *Humour*,
that cannot meet with any Objection
even from the most Rigid among us :
But whether incapacitated by Illness,
or over-ruled by the Sweetness of his
Temper, (which *your Lordship* knows
he has an Excess of,) he trusts entirely
to these Men, who by the bad Plays,
which they revive, and by mangling
the good ones, which they sometimes
act, shew they have no Ability to con-
trive for the *Stage* ; tho' they are really
very good *Actors*, and have it in their
power, by their Talents that way, to
make the *Theatre* highly diverting, if
they would confine it to *Acting*.

ONE would think their Gratitude
(if they have any thing worthy in
them,) should give them a little more
Com-

Complaisance for the *Nobility* and *Gentry*, who have show'd so much Indulgence to them: But if they will not oblige them in what is most desir'd, and in what they most excel, the Town can never be blamed for deserting them for the other House, who are vastly superiour to them in these *Entertainments*.

If we have many such debauch'd sickly Minds, that have lost their true Relish for *Wit* and *Sense*, and cannot be pleas'd but with these *Absurdities*, they may be indulg'd, but not at the expence of those of a better *Taste*. Those of the New House may content themselves with these Follies; they have always (it must be said to their praise,) done their utmost to divert by their Acting, but they find it impossible: In them therefore it is obliging, in the others it is impudent; in them it is Prudence, in the others it is Madness.

But

BUT I will not trouble *your Lord-ship* any further with these Men; I believe my LORD CHAMBERLAIN (I know it is generally expected, and I was told so by *Lord S......*) resolves to exert his Authority, and to let them see, they are not the only *Judges*, what is proper for the *Stage*: I cannot think it any way beneath his *Grace's* Notice, if *Comedy* has that happy Power to laugh Men out of their Vices and Follies, we are not so perfect, but it may be still of consequence; we have our *Foplings*, a few of them, and indeed some little Variety of *Fools*, who are good-natur'd enough to expose themselves for the Improvement of *Satire*.

IF *Tragedy* is (as I think ARISTOTLE calls it,) a living *Lecture*, infinitely more instructive than *Philosophy*, abstracting the *Charms* of it, it merits the Consideration of every Man for its *Use*.

MR.

Mr. Addison (and there never was a better Judge, or a finer Taste,) says, that one of the greatest Pleasures, the Mind is capable of receiving, is given by a well-written *Tragedy* : It wears out (says he) every thing that is *mean* and *little* in us, it cultivates that *Humanity*, which is the Ornament of our *Nature* ; it softens *Insolence*, sooths *Affliction*, and subdues us to the Dispensations of *Providence*. It is therefore surely worthy of his *Grace*, to keep our *Theatre* from being a *Scandal* to our *Nation*, since it has hitherto been an *Honour* to it.

I Am satisfy'd by this time *your Lordship* wishes you had not reproach'd me for the Shortness of my Letters : Indeed, *my Lord*, you had more reason to blame me for the Negligence of them ; for, correct as you are yourself, you find, your Example has not

had

had the happy Influence on me it should have had.

I THINK I am sufficiently reveng'd on *your Lordship* for the Sharpness of your Upbraidings; and therefore will relieve you with some Lines, that are handed about on one of the present *Amusements*, call'd APOLLO *and* DAPHNE: They are but in very few hands, they were written by *your Lordship's* old Acquaintance Mr........ and given me by *Lady R* .... with her Desire to send them to *your Lordship* with her *Devoir*, and to let you know, she is more than ever an Enemy to the Country, since it deprives her of *your Lordship's* Visits.

I am,

MY DEAR LORD,

Most unfeignedly,

the Sincerest of your Servants.

 Etir'd from Noise, beneath a pleasing Shad
For soft Repose, and pensive Quiet mad

With *Love*, the only Torment in my Breast,

Yet *Love* at length resigning me to Rest:

In balmy Sleep to find that Peace I try'd,

Which my CORINNA's Cruelty deny'd.

When strait a *Form* appears, each blooming Grac

Unfading Youth, and Beauty in his Face;

Eternal Rays, which round his Temples shine,

Dazling with Light, confess the *Form* Divine.

APOLI

APOLLO ſpake, and at each Word he frown'd;

Ÿet ſweet each Word, melodious ev'ry Sound.

Miſtaken *Britons* ! thoughtleſs and unwiſe !

Slaves to each Fool ! betray'd by ev'ry Vice !

You ! whom, diſtinguiſh'd from Mankind, I've grac'd

With ev'ry Gift, with ev'ry Science bleſs'd :

With *Muſic* have adorn'd the Fair-One's Tongue,

(Her Eyes are not ſo dang'rous as her Song :)

In pity to Your Cares, inſpir'd with *Skill*

The *Poet's* Breaſt, and taught him to excel :

For You, I gave my SHAKESPEAR ev'ry Art,

With Fear to chill, with Fire to warm the Heart :

For You I gave my OTWAY ev'ry Charm

To raiſe Your Griefs, and then thoſe Griefs diſarm :

" For

" For You I fram'd my C O N G R E V E to delight

" With flowing Humour, unaffected Wit.

" My A D D I S O N and S T E E L E I form'd to plea

" To judge with Candor, ridicule with Eafe.

" My H U G H E S---But here a Tear ftole gently dow

And loft in filent Grief, He ceas'd to frown:

Mourning, as Mortal for a Friend, He ftood,

But with his Speech He foon refum'd the G O D.

" For You I've nourifh'd up a Youthful Train,

" With Strength to fing, with Sweetnefs in ea

    Strain :

" With ev'ry Grace, with ev'ry Pow'r to move,

" The Senfe to ravifh, and the Soul improve:

" For You,---but You ungrateful to the *Mufe*,

" Contemn her Precepts, and her Charms refufe.

                  " Wra

Wrapt in Attention to each Nonsense sit,

And spurn at nought but Virtue, or at Wit.

Unthinking!——but unworthy my Reproof!

No,——Your own Folly's Punishment enough.

How can you bear to see unskilful Men

Your *God* of *Verse*, your once lov'd *God* prophane?

Shall they, whose Trade is Wit, its Pow'r disown?

Nay, make its *God* conspire, and turn *Buffoon?*

Shall impious *Mercenaries* dare t'expose

The Errors of a *God* in senseless Shows?

DAPHNE I lov'd, but she my Love withstood,

Severely Chaste, and obstinately Good:

In vain the *Nymph* my Youth, my Beauty view'd,

In vain with all the Force of Wit I su'd,

" In

" In vain I fung,——and tho' divine each Strain,

" Stay DAPHNE,—DAPHNE fled——I fung in vain.

" Since *Youth*, fince *Beauty*, *Wit* and *Mufic* fail'd,

" What! could they think fhe'd to a *Dancer* yield?

" Where's my lov'd POPE? Can POPE contented fe

" Thefe vile Abufers of the Sex and Me?

" Beauty and Wit fhould be his darling Care,

" His Song's the Pleafure of the Wife and Fair.

" Where's YOUNG? YOUNG glows with a Poet

     Rage,

" YOUNG can correct thefe *Triflers* of the *Stage*

" Why fleep my Sons? why flumbers ev'ry Pen?

" Shall *Folly* licens'd thus triumphant reign?

" Why fleep my Sons? the Caufe is Yours, arife,

" *Folly* ne'er triumphs, but when *Virtue* dies.

         E   " W

" Who firſt ſhall dare theſe *Monſters* to engage,

" Who firſt ſhall chaſe theſe *Trifles* from the Stage,

' Who firſt ſhall dare to riſe in *Wit's* Defence,

" Theſe *Wretches* ſcourge, and laſh them into Senſe;

' My fav'rite *Laurel* ſhall adorn his Brow,

' His *Honours* ſhall increaſe as that ſhall grow,

And I no more bewail my DRYDEN or my ROWE.

F I N I S.